First World War
and Army of Occupation
War Diary
France, Belgium and Germany

51 DIVISION
Divisional Troops
Divisional Cyclist Company
1 May 1915 - 30 April 1916

WO95/2854/2

The Naval & Military Press Ltd
www.nmarchive.com
Published in association with The National Archives

Published by

The Naval & Military Press Ltd

Unit 10 Ridgewood Industrial Park,

Uckfield, East Sussex,

TN22 5QE England

Tel: +44 (0) 1825 749494

www.naval-military-press.com

www.nmarchive.com

This diary has been reprinted in facsimile from the original. Any imperfections are inevitably reproduced and the quality may fall short of modern type and cartographic standards.

© **Crown Copyright**
Images reproduced by permission of The National Archives, London, England, 2015.

Contents

Document type	Place/Title	Date From	Date To
Heading	WO95/2854/2 51 Div. Divnl Cyclist Co 1915 May-1916 April		
Heading	51st Division 51st Divl Cyclist Coy May 1915-Apr 1916		
Heading	51st Division 51st Cyclist Coy. Vol I 1-31.5.15		
War Diary	Cardington	01/05/1915	01/05/1915
War Diary	WB Havre	02/05/1915	02/05/1915
War Diary	France	03/05/1915	03/05/1915
War Diary	Busnes	04/05/1915	13/05/1915
War Diary	Pradelles	14/05/1915	18/05/1915
War Diary	La Gorgue	19/05/1915	19/05/1915
War Diary	Les Choquaux	20/05/1915	31/05/1915
Heading	51st Division 51st Dist. Cyclist Coy. Vol II 1-30.6.15		
War Diary	Hinges	01/06/1915	02/06/1915
War Diary	Locon	03/06/1915	27/06/1915
War Diary	Le Nouveau Monde	28/06/1915	30/06/1915
Heading	51st Division 51st Cyclist Coy. Vol III 1-31.7.15		
War Diary	Le Nouveau Monde	01/07/1915	27/07/1915
War Diary	Heilly	28/07/1915	30/07/1915
War Diary	Martinsart	30/07/1915	31/07/1915
Heading	51st Divl. Cyclist Coy Vol IV From 1-31.8.15		
War Diary	Martinsart	01/08/1915	08/08/1915
War Diary	Buire	09/08/1915	31/08/1915
Heading	51st Division 51st Divl. Cyclist Coy Vol V Sept 15		
War Diary	Buire	01/09/1915	15/09/1915
War Diary	Baizieux	16/09/1915	30/09/1915
Heading	51st Division 51st Divl Cyclist Co. Oct-15 Vol VI		
War Diary	Baizieux	01/10/1915	31/10/1915
Heading	51st Divl Cyclist Co. Nov 1915 Vol VII		
War Diary	Baizieux	01/11/1915	30/11/1915
Heading	51st Divl Cyclist Co. Dec Vol VIII 121/7929		
War Diary	Baizieux	01/12/1915	26/12/1915
War Diary	Mirvaux	27/12/1915	31/12/1915
Heading	51st Divl Cyclist Co. Jan IX		
War Diary	Mirvaux	01/01/1916	07/02/1916
War Diary	Daours	08/02/1916	29/02/1916
Heading	51 Cyclist Coy Vol XI		
War Diary	Flesselles	01/03/1916	05/03/1916
War Diary	Hardinval	06/03/1916	07/03/1916
War Diary	Oppy	08/03/1916	08/03/1916
War Diary	Maroeuil	09/03/1916	10/03/1916
War Diary	Trenches	11/03/1916	16/03/1916
War Diary	Reserve Trenches	17/03/1916	17/03/1916
War Diary	Roclincourt	18/03/1916	21/03/1916
War Diary	Front Trenches	22/03/1916	28/03/1916
War Diary	Hermaville	29/03/1916	31/03/1916
Heading	51 Cyclist Coy Vol XII		
War Diary	Hermaville	01/04/1916	15/04/1916
War Diary	Maroeuil Trenches	16/04/1916	22/04/1916
War Diary	Hermaville	23/04/1916	30/04/1916

WO 95 2854/2

51 Div: Divnl Cyclist Co
1915 May – 1916 April

51ST DIVISION

51ST DIVL CYCLIST COY
MAY 1915-APR 1916

2709

12/5505

51st Division.

51st Polish Coy.

Vol I 1 — 31.5.15.

No. IX

Army Form C. 2118.

WAR DIARY
or
INTELLIGENCE SUMMARY.
(Erase heading not required.)

Instructions regarding War Diaries and Intelligence Summaries are contained in F. S. Regs., Part II. and the Staff Manual respectively. Title pages will be prepared in manuscript.

Place	Date	Hour	Summary of Events and Information	Remarks and references to Appendices
CARDINGTON	1/5/15	9 A.M.	Prepared for departure. Strength on leaving CARDINGTON 190 men & 8 Officers including two men attached from R.A.M.C. and two men attached from A.S.C.	WD3.
HAVRE	2/5/15	7 A.M.	Disembarked HAVRE at 7 A.M. Entrained at 7.30 P.M. Departed at 11.30 P.M.	WD3
"	"	"	Estafette joined us at HAVRE	WD3
FRANCE	3/5/15		Spent day in Train	WD3
BUSNES	4/5/15	10 P.M.	Detrained BERGUETTE at 10 P.M. Marched to BUSNES and billeted. Interior economy and company training	WD3 WD3
D°	5/5/15		" " " "	WD3
D°	6/5/15		" " " "	WD3
D°	7/5/15		" " " "	WD3
D°	8/5/15		" " " " H.D. Op. Order 2 received	WD3
D°	9/5/15		Company stood by awaiting orders. Three officers & patrols reconnoitred roads leading to VIEILLE CHAPELLE and BOUT DEVILLE	WD3
D°	10/5/15		Company stood by awaiting orders. Interior economy	WD3
D°	11/5/15		Company training and interior economy	WD3

Army Form C. 2118.

WAR DIARY
or
INTELLIGENCE SUMMARY.
(Erase heading not required.)

Instructions regarding War Diaries and Intelligence Summaries are contained in F.S. Regs., Part II. and the Staff Manual respectively. Title pages will be prepared in manuscript.

Place	Date	Hour	Summary of Events and Information	Remarks and references to Appendices
BUSNES	12/5/15		Name of unit changed to 51st (Highland) Cyclist Company. Company training	WB
Do	13/5/15		Interior economy. Weather very rainy. Received orders to be in readiness to march off at 8.30 A.M. on 14/5/15 in a northerly direction.	WB
PRADELLES	14/5/15		Departed from BUSNES for PRADELLES at 8.30	WB
Do	15/5/15		Interior economy and company training	WB
Do	16/5/15		Church parade at 12 NOON	WB
Do	17/5/15		Company training	WB
Do	18/5/15		Do	WB
LA GORGUE	19/5/15		Departed from PRADELLES at 6 A.M. arrived in LA GORGUE at 9 A.M.	WB
LES CHOQUAUX	20/5/15		Departed from LA GORGUE at 10 A.M. arrived at LES CHOQUAUX at 11.30 A.M.	WB
Do	20/5/15		Interior economy	WB
Do	21/5/15		Order received to detail one N.C.O. and nine men to report to O.C. Signals at ADVANCED HEADQUARTERS 51st (HIGHLAND) Division at 11 A.M. on the 22nd to act as cyclist orderlies. — Company training	WB

Army Form C. 2118.

WAR DIARY
or
INTELLIGENCE SUMMARY.
(Erase heading not required.)

Instructions regarding War Diaries and Intelligence Summaries are contained in F. S. Regs., Part II. and the Staff Manual respectively. Title pages will be prepared in manuscript.

Place	Date	Hour	Summary of Events and Information	Remarks and references to Appendices
LES CHOQUAUX	22/5/15		Interior Economy & Company training. Two men detailed to guide draft of 40 men from MERVILLE to HEADQUARTERS at LOCON	WT3
	23/5/15		Removed to billets about half a mile N.W. of former billet. Lance Corporal and two men sent to ADVANCED HEADQUARTERS to increase detachment there. Company training	WT3
	24/5/15		Company training	WT3
	25/5/15		2/Lt A.P. TAYLOR detailed to attend a 24 hour course in Gas Bombs. Cyclist detailed to report daily at the FIELD POST OFFICE, LOCON to carry in mail to and from MERVILLE	WT3
	26/5/15		Company training	WT3
	27/5/15		One cyclist from No 1 Platoon returned from HEADQUARTERS killed at LACOUTURE	WT3
	28/5/15		Company training. Seven men returned from Gas Bomb Course. at LOCON. 24 men detailed for Gas Bomb Course.	WT3
	29/5/15		Company training. Seven men detailed from No 3 Platoon to relieve men at DIVISIONAL HEADQUARTERS, LOCON.	WT3

Army Form C. 2118.

WAR DIARY
or
INTELLIGENCE SUMMARY.
(Erase heading not required.)

Instructions regarding War Diaries and Intelligence Summaries are contained in F. S. Regs., Part II. and the Staff Manual respectively. Title pages will be prepared in manuscript.

Place	Date	Hour	Summary of Events and Information	Remarks and references to Appendices
LES CHOQUAUX	24/3/15		Interior economy	WD 4473
	31/3/15		Company training	4473

121/5829

51ˢᵗ Division.

51ˢᵗ Div: Gydysh Coy.

Part II 1 – 30.6.15

WAR DIARY
or
INTELLIGENCE SUMMARY.
(Erase heading not required.)

Army Form C. 2118.

Place	Date	Hour	Summary of Events and Information	Remarks and references to Appendices
HINGES	1/6/15		Company Training & Interior Economy.	W.S.
"	2/6/15		do. Orders for Company to proceed to LOCON on following day. Four Officers (Capt. ROGERSON, 2Lt. McWILLIAM, 2Lt. DOIG, 2Lt. BIRNIE) detailed for duty with Engineers at LE TOURET.	W.S.
LOCON	3/6/15	10 AM	Arrived at new billets at LOCON. Lt. ROBERTSON returned to his unit 3rd Gordons. Company training. No 1 Platoon joined Eng. were in trenches for instructional purposes in Communication trenches Sk.	W.S.
"	4/6/15	7.30 AM	½ Coy proceeded to trenches with ENGINEERS.	W.S.
"	5/6/15	"	do. 2 Sections attaches to 7/11 High. Field Coy R.E 2/2	W.S.
"	6/6/15	"	2 " " Oth. ½ Coy in trenches	W.S.
"	6/6/15	"	do. do	W.S.
"	7/6/15	"	do. do	W.S.
"	8/6/15	"	do.	W.S.
"	9/6/15	9.30 AM	Instruction from ENGINEERS.	W.S.
		7.30 PM	½ Coy in trenches.	W.S.

WAR DIARY
or
INTELLIGENCE SUMMARY.

(Erase heading not required.)

Army Form C. 2118.

Instructions regarding War Diaries and Intelligence Summaries are contained in F. S. Regs., Part II. and the Staff Manual respectively. Title pages will be prepared in manuscript.

Place	Date	Hour	Summary of Events and Information	Remarks and references to Appendices
LOCON	10/6/15	9.30PM	Instruction from Engineers. ½ Coy in trenches from 9.30 PM – 1.30 AM.	W.S.
"	11/6/15		do	W.S.
"	12/6/15		do	W.S.
"	13/6/15	9.30	do	W.S.
"		11 AM	Divine Service conducted by Major Sinclair.	W.S.
"	14/6/15	9.30 PM	Instruction from Engineers. ½ Coy in trenches.	W.S.
"	15/6/15		do	W.S.
"	16/6/15		do	W.S.
"	17/6/15		do	W.S.
"	18/6/15		do	W.S.
"		11.30 PM	One man wounded in shoulder whilst in trenches	W.S.
"	19/6/15	9.30 PM	Instruction from Engineers. ½ Coy in trenches.	W.S.
"	20/6/15	9.30	do	W.S.
"		11 AM	Divine Service conducted by Major Sinclair	W.S.
"	21/6/15	9 AM	2 additional men detailed to Signal Coy for duty. ½ Coy in trenches	W.S.
"	22/6/15		Instruction from Engineers. ½ Coy in trenches.	W.S.

WAR DIARY
or
INTELLIGENCE SUMMARY.
(Erase heading not required.)

Army Form C. 2118.

Place	Date	Hour	Summary of Events and Information	Remarks and references to Appendices
LOCON	23/6/15	9 A.M.	Instructor from Engineers. ½ Coy. in trenches for 24 hours.	M.S.
"	24/6/15	9 P.M.	do - do -	M.S.
"	"	10 A.M.	1 man killed & 1 man wounded in trenches.	M.S.
			F.G.C. Martial of Pte R. LAIRD 3378. on a charge of "When on active service disobeying a lawful command given by his superior Officer." Pres. MAJOR J.W. CARDEN 1st/8th HIGH. F.A. BRIGADE	
			Members. Capt. W.D. BARRATT. 1/4 Bn. R. LANCASTER R.M.	M.S.
			Lt. A.P. TAYLOR 51st (High) Div. CYCLIST. COY. R.M.	M.S.
"	25/6/15	9 A.M.	½ Coy in trenches. Heavy rains -	M.S.
"	26/6/15	"	do -	M.S.
"	"	4.30 P.	Promulgation of sentence on Pte R. LAIRD 3378 by Capt. ROGERSON. Sentence 84 days Field Punishment No 1 commuted to 56 days by Major General ALLISON Commanding HIGH. DIVISION.	M.S.
"	27/6/15	9 A.M.	Orders to proceed to LE NOUVEAU MONDE.	M.S.
LE NOUVEAU	"	4.30 P.M.	Coy. arrived at new billet as per orders. 2nd QM. McWilliam admitted to Hospital.	M.S.
MONDE	28/6/15	9.30.	Company Training, 4 men detailed to DHQrs. for duty.	M.S.

Army Form C. 2118.

WAR DIARY
or
INTELLIGENCE SUMMARY.
(Erase heading not required.)

Instructions regarding War Diaries and Intelligence Summaries are contained in F. S. Regs., Part II. and the Staff Manual respectively. Title pages will be prepared in manuscript.

Place	Date	Hour	Summary of Events and Information	Remarks and references to Appendices
Le Nouveau Monde	29/6/15	8pm	Company Training. 2 Sections with 2/2 H.F. Coy. R.E. in trenches.	W.S.-
"	30/6/15		Company Training.	W.S.-

51st Division

61st Cyclist Coy.
Vol III 1 — 31.7.15.

17/6714

Army Form C. 2118.

WAR DIARY
or
INTELLIGENCE SUMMARY.

(Erase heading not required.)

WAR DIARY OF 51st H. Div. Cyclist Coy JULY.

Instructions regarding War Diaries and Intelligence Summaries are contained in F. S. Regs., Part II. and the Staff Manual respectively. Title pages will be prepared in manuscript.

Place	Date	Hour	Summary of Events and Information	Remarks and references to Appendices
Le Nouveau Monde	July 1		Company Training. Men acting as guides to reinforcing parties and convalescents.	
"	2.	5pm	3 Sections with 2/2 H.7.Coy R.E. in trenches	
			Company Training. Reconnoitring Defence Scheme of Divisional Area.	
"	3	8.15"	3 Sections with 2/2 R.E. in trenches.	
			Reconnoitring Strong posts. 30 men & 1 officer assisting 1/1 R.E. in digging	
		8.30"	instruction trench. 3 Sections with 1/2 R.E.	
"	4		Company Training. Reconnoitring Strong Posts.	
			50 men with 1/1 R.E. digging Reserve trench. 3 Sections with 2/2 R.E.	
		8.30"	Company Training. Reconnoitring Strong Posts.	
"	5	8.15"	3 Sections with 2/2 R.E. & 2 Sections with 1/1 R.E.	
"	6	9.30 am	Reconnoitring Defence Scheme of Div. Area. 2 Sections with 1/1 R.E. trenches	
		2 pm	Strong post. 2 Sections with 2/2 R.E. to assist in repairing Strong post.	
		5.30"	2 Sections with 1/1 R.E. in trenches.	
			Captain Cox reported himself for duty.	

1577 Wt.W10791/1773 500,000 1/15 D. D. & L. A.D.S.S./Forms/C. 2118.

Army Form C. 2118.

WAR DIARY
or
INTELLIGENCE SUMMARY.
(Erase heading not required.)

Instructions regarding War Diaries and Intelligence Summaries are contained in F. S. Regs., Part II. and the Staff Manual respectively. Title pages will be prepared in manuscript.

Place	Date	Hour	Summary of Events and Information	Remarks and references to Appendices
Le Nouveau Monde	July 7	9.30 AM	2 Sections with ½ R.E. 2 Sections with ½ R.E.	WS
		2 pm	2 Sections with ½ R.E.	WS
		8.30	2 Sections with ½ R.E. 2 Sections with ½ R.E.	WS
"	8	9.30 AM	2 Sections with ½ R.E. 2 Sections with ½ R.E.	
		2.30 pm	2 " "	WS
		9 pm	2 " "	
"	9	9.30 AM	2 Sections with ½ R.E. 2 Sections with ½ R.E. Company Training.	
		2.30 pm	2 " "	
	10	9.30 AM	4 Sections with R.E.	WS
		5 pm	½ Coy at Baths in LA COGRUE.	
"	11	9.30 AM	2 Sections with ½ R.E.	
		4 pm	Church Service.	
	12	8.30 pm	1 Section with ½ R.E. + 1 Section with ½ R.E.	WS
		9.30	Working with R.E.	
		8.30 pm	2 Sections with ½ R.E.	
"	13	9.30	6 Sections with R.E. by day and 2 Sections by night. One Corporal wounded in neck.	WS

Army Form C. 2118.

Instructions regarding War Diaries and Intelligence Summaries are contained in F. S. Regs., Part II. and the Staff Manual respectively. Title pages will be prepared in manuscript.

WAR DIARY
or
INTELLIGENCE SUMMARY.
(Erase heading not required.)

Place	Date	Hour	Summary of Events and Information	Remarks and references to Appendices
LE NOUVEAU MONDE	JULY 13		CAPT. ROGERSON returned from R.E. for duty with CYCLIST. COY CAPT. COX went to R.E. for duty.	A/S
"	14		6 Sections with R.E. by day + 2 Sections by night. Corporal wounded on the 12th dies of wounds.	A/S
"	15		4 Sections by day with R.E + 3 Sections by night.	
"	16		F.G.Court Martial of No 3222 Pte J. MCINTYRE for displaying a taught command given by his Superior officer. Resident MAJOR Hon. A HAMILTON RUSSELL D SQUADRON NORTH IRISH HORSE Members CAPT. A.T. DAWSON 3rd H.F.A. (How) BRIGADE AMMN COLUMN. Lt. A.P. TAYLOR 51st/4 Dv CYCLIST COY.	A/S
"	17	6pm	CAPT COX returned to CYCLIST COY for duty. Promulgation of F.G.C Martial Sentence. 4 2 days F.P. Punishment No 1	A/S
"	18		2 Sections with R.E. Church Service: Private wounded in leg.	
"	19		Private wounded. Company training.	
"	20		4 Sections with R.E. by day + night.	A/S
"	21		F.G.C.M. Sentence on Pte J MCINTYRE quashed through irregularity of procedure Interior Economy.	

Army Form C. 2118.

WAR DIARY
or
INTELLIGENCE SUMMARY.
(Erase heading not required.)

Place	Date	Hour	Summary of Events and Information	Remarks and references to Appendices
LE NOUVEAU MONDE	JULY 22		Company Training. Interior Economy. Orders to proceed to new billets on following day	WS
"	23	4 pm	Proceeded to new billets at BEAUPRÉ [Sheet 36A. 32.C.98.]	WS
			Lt A.P. TAYLOR & platoon left on cycles for new divisional area near Amiens to report to MAJOR NICHOLSON on SUNDAY morning.	WS
	24		Recconoitering & Company training.	
	25	5 pm	Bathing Parade.	WS
	26		Company training. Orders to leave on 27th for new billets.	WS
			do	WS
	27	4.45 pm	Vehicles entrained at LA GORGUE STATION.	WS
		6.45 pm	Personnel " " " "	WS
			One man accidentally killed & one man accidentally injured at CORBIE STATION whilst helping to detrain transport with SIGNAL Coy.	WS
HEILLY	28	8.45 am	Arrived at CORBIE STATION. Detained & cycled to HEILLY about 11 miles distant	WS
"	29	12 AM	Received orders to proceed to MARTINSART but these were cancelled at 4 pm	WS

WAR DIARY
or
INTELLIGENCE SUMMARY.

(Erase heading not required.)

Army Form C. 2118.

Place	Date	Hour	Summary of Events and Information	Remarks and references to Appendices
HEILLY	JULY 29		Capt. Cox attached reported to A.P.M. for duty. 2Lt Birnie returned for duty from 1/1 R.E. 2Lt McWilliam returned to Cyclist Coy from 1/1 R.E. for duty.	1/RE/WS WS
"	30	3 pm	2Lt Doig, 2Lt McWilliam, 2Lt Birnie, and 100 men left for Martinsart.	
"			Lt Doig 2Lt McWilliam, 2Lt Birnie, Headquarters at 6 pm. to report at Brigade Headquarters at 6 pm.	WS
"		7 pm	Capt. Rogerson. Lt Taylor & 2Lt Smith. remainder of Coy left for Ross Roads S of B.S Bowl to report to O.C. 5th Seaforths at 8.30 pm.	WS
MARTINSART		10 pm	Arrived at Martinsart. Lt Doig, 2Lt McWilliam, 2Lt Birnie + 100 men left for trenches with 6th Seaforths. The remainder of the Coy remained in billets at Martinsart.	
"	31	12 noon	Remainder of Coy still at Martinsart	WS

51ˢᵗ Division

12/6598

51ˢᵗ Divl: Cyclist Coy

Vol IV

From 1 – 31. 8. 15

Mi:

Army Form C. 2118.

WAR DIARY
or
~~INTELLIGENCE~~ SUMMARY. of 51st DIV. CYCLIST. COY.
for month of AUGUST.

(Erase heading not required.)

Instructions regarding War Diaries and Intelligence Summaries are contained in F.S. Regs., Part II. and the Staff Manual respectively. Title pages will be prepared in manuscript.

Place	Date	Hour	Summary of Events and Information	Remarks and references to Appendices
MARTINSART	Aug. 1	10 pm	2/3 Coy in trenches with "A" Coy 1/6 SEAFORTH HLGS. at THIEPVAL.	W.S.
"	2		1/3 Coy at MARTINSART	W.S.
"	3		do. Lce Sgt. SUTHERLAND wounded by himself.	W.S.
"			2Lt BIRNIE returned with 50 men from trenches to MARTINSART. and 2Lt McWILLIAM	
"	4	10 pm	1st SMITH took 50 men to trenches from "	W.S.
"			1 man accidentally wounded in trenches.	
"	5		2/3 Coy in trenches & 1/3 Coy at billets in MARTINSART do.	W.S.
"	6	10 pm	Lt DOIG & 2Lt McWILLIAM left trenches with 30 men & Lt TAYLOR & 2Lt BIRNIE took 50 men to trenches.	W.S.
"	7	5 am	1 man killed in trenches by sniper. CAPT ROGERSON went on leave to ENGLAND for 8 days.	W.S.
"	8	4 pm	Coy left trenches & proceeded to MARTINSART - when it got instructions to leave for BUIRE where it arrived at 11 p.m. Reinforcement of 3 men from SCOTLAND	W.S.
BUIRE	9		Interior Economy. CAPT COX got instruction to take command of 4th DIV. CYCLIST COY on 10th. Reinforcement of 2 men from SCOTLAND	W.S.

WAR DIARY
or
INTELLIGENCE SUMMARY.
(Erase heading not required.)

Army Form C. 2118.

Place	Date	Hour	Summary of Events and Information	Remarks and references to Appendices
BUIRE	Aug 10	2 pm	Interior Economy. Lts DOIG & BIRNIE with ½ Coy joined 2/½ R.E at ALBERT.	W.S
"	11		Company training. ½ Coy with R.E at ALBERT.	W.S
"	12		do	
"	13	?	do	
"			F.G.C.M of 3782 L/Sgt. SUTHERLAND & 2445 PRIVATE KNOWLES on Charges of Disgraceful conduct in that they while on the march wilfully maimed themselves by firing a bullet through the forefinger of the right hand with intent thereby to render themselves unfit for service. 2nd Charge to the prejudice of good order military discipline in that they while in the trenches carelessly handled a loaded rifle in such a manner as to cause themselves injury. PRIVATE KNOWLES acquitted.	W.S
"	14		Lt TAYLOR at F.G.C.M. ½ Coy with Engineers - 3 NCOs, 40 men at RIBEMONT with R.E.	W.S
"	15	5.30	½ Coy with R.E at ALBERT. CHURCH SERVICE by Major SINCLAIR.	W.S
"	16		do Company training.	W.S
"	17		do Capt ROGERSON returned to duty.	W.S
"	18	9.30 pm	Instructions received that Coy was in reserve for 152nd BRIGADE in trenches. ½ Coy with R.E. Company training.	W.S
"	19	9 am	2nd Lt SMITH & 50 men fatigue party to FRENCH mining Coy at LA BOISELLE	W.S
"	20		½ Coy with R.E. - Company training.	
"	21		Lt TAYLOR went on leave. Interior Economy.	W.S

WAR DIARY
or
INTELLIGENCE SUMMARY.

(Erase heading not required.)

Army Form C. 2118.

Place	Date	Hour	Summary of Events and Information	Remarks and references to Appendices
BOIRE	Aug 22	8.30	½ Coy with ½ R.E. at ALBERT. Interior Economy. 2/Lt HOWIE reported for duty.	W/D
"	23	"	" Company Training -	do -
"	24	"	"	do
"	25	"	"	do
"	26	"	"	do -
"	27	6 pm	Promulgation of F.G.C.M. sentence on L Sgt SUTHERLAND. Found guilty on Second Charge. Punishment - Reduced to ranks, 7 days F.P No 1. 14 days stoppage of pay. ½ Coy with ½ R.E. repairing billets -	do -
"	28	8.30	½ Coy with ½ R.E. at ALBERT. ½ Coy repairing billets.	"
"	29	"	"	
"	30	3 pm	Church Service by Rev Capt DONALD. Lt TAYLOR returned from leave. ½ Coy with R.E. ½ Coy repairing billets	do -
"	31	"	½ Coy with R.E. ½ Coy repairing billets do	

51st/15 train

121/6918

51st Div: Cyclist Coy
Vol V
Sept. 15

WAR DIARY of 51st Divisional Cyclist Coy.

INTELLIGENCE SUMMARY.

for month of SEPTEMBER.

(Erase heading not required.)

Army Form C. 2118.

Place	Date	Hour	Summary of Events and Information	Remarks and references to Appendices
BUIRE	SEPT. 1		½ Coy with 2/2 R.E. at ALBERT. ½ Coy repairing billets	WS.
	2		do do	WS.
	3		do do	WS.
	4		do do	WS.
	5	4/pm	do do (Church Service.)	WS.
	6		do do	WS.
	7		do do	WS.
	8		do do	WS.
	9		do do	WS.
	10		do do	WS.
	11		do do	WS.
	12		do do	WS.
	13		do do	WS.
	14		do do	WS.
	15		Orders to proceed to BAIZIEUX the following afternoon	WS

Army Form C. 2118.

WAR DIARY
or
INTELLIGENCE SUMMARY.
(Erase heading not required.)

of 51st Divisional Cyclist Company for month of September

Place	Date	Hour	Summary of Events and Information	Remarks and references to Appendices
Baizieux	16	3pm	Arrived at Baizieux. ½ Coy with 1/1 RE at Bouzin Court. ½ Coy digging Sandpits at Baizieux	WS
"	17		do	WS
"	18		do	WS
"	19		Church Service conducted by Major Sinclair.	WS
"	20		do	WS
"	21		do	WS
"	22		do	WS
"	23		Tactical Scheme with North Irish Horse	WS
"	24	10.30am	2Lt McWilliam & "L" Howie with 50 men at Avelny with 1/1 RE. Farewell message from General Bannatyne-Allason 51st Division	WS
"	25		Interior Economy. ½ Coy digging sand at Baizieux. Message from Sir John French to troops	WS
"	26		Church Service conducted by Major Sinclair. Reinforcements 1 Corp and 13 men. Digging sand	WS

Army Form C. 2118.

WAR DIARY
or
INTELLIGENCE SUMMARY.
(Erase heading not required.)

Place	Date	Hour	Summary of Events and Information	Remarks and references to Appendices
BAIZIEUX	27		½ Coy with R.E. at BOUZINCOURT. ½ Coy sand digging.	W.S.
"	28		do. do.	W.S.
"	29		do. Superior Economy.	W.S.
"	30		do. do.	

51ˢᵗ Kurbrin

51ˢᵗ Div Cyclac Co.

Oct. 15

VI von

121/4498

Army Form C. 2118.

WAR DIARY
or
INTELLIGENCE SUMMARY of 51st Div. Cyclist Coy. for October.

(Erase heading not required.)

Place	Date	Hour	Summary of Events and Information	Remarks and references to Appendices
BAIZIEUX	Oct. 1		2Lt BIRNIE transferred to R. ENGINEERS. Lt TAYLOR promoted CAPTAIN.	W.S.
"	2		½ Coy with R.E. ½ Coy making bath house & drying room. & working at Sand pit.	W.S.
"	3		do. DIVINE SERVICE Conducted by Major Sinclair	W.S.
"	4		do.	W.S.
"	5		do.	W.S.
"	6		Company Training. Tactical Scheme – "Working at Sand pit."	W.S.
"	7		do. Flank Guard Scheme. "	W.S.
"	8		do. Convoy Scheme "	W.S.
"	9		do. Tactical Scheme "	W.S.
"	10	4.30pm	Coy inspected by G.O.C. MAJOR GENERAL HARPER	W.S.
"	11		Interior Economy. Church service by Major Sinclair	W.S.
"	12		Tactical Scheme. Attack on village of HARPONVILLE	W.S.
"	13		Interior Economy. Bathing Parade.	W.S.
"	14		½ Coy with R.E. Interior Economy. 2Lt McWilliam went on leave to Sen-	

WAR DIARY or INTELLIGENCE SUMMARY.

Army Form C. 2118.

(Erase heading not required.)

Place	Date	Hour	Summary of Events and Information	Remarks and references to Appendices
BAIZIEUX	Oct 15		½ Coy with R.E. Interior Economy & Coy training.	
"	16		do	
"	17		2/3 Coy with R.E. at BOUZINCOURT.	
"	~~17~~		Church Service by Major SINCLAIR. 2 Lt GRANT reported for duty.	W.S
"	18		Company Training.	
"	19		2/3 Coy with R.E. Lt DOIG transferred to R.E.	W.S.
"	20	12.30	119 men & 2 Officers with R.E. in trenches.	
"	21		do. 2 Lt CROOKS reported for duty.	
"	22		1 man killed in trenches.	W.S.
"	23		1 Officer & 60 men at Railhead with R.E. Coy training.	
"	24		1 Officer & 80 men at RIBEMONT with R.E. Working at sandpit.	W.S.
"	25		3 Officers & Coy. with R.E. at trenches.	
"	26		do	
"	27		Company Training	
"	28		2/3 Coy with R.E. at BOUZINCOURT. do	W.S.

Army Form C. 2118.

WAR DIARY
or
INTELLIGENCE SUMMARY.
(Erase heading not required.)

Instructions regarding War Diaries and Intelligence Summaries are contained in F. S. Regs., Part II. and the Staff Manual respectively. Title pages will be prepared in manuscript.

Place	Date	Hour	Summary of Events and Information	Remarks and references to Appendices
BAIZIEUX	Oct 29		2/3 Coy with R.E. at BOUZINCOURT	1st.
"	30		Coy with R.E. at henches	10th.
"	31		2/3 Coy with R.E. at BOUZINCOURT. 2Lt SMITH went on leave to SCOTLAND.	10th.

121/7636

III

Nov '15

Sind Cycline Co.

51/9%

WAR DIARY of 51st DIVISIONAL CYCLIST COY
or
INTELLIGENCE SUMMARY.
(Erase heading not required.) for NOVEMBER.

Army Form C. 2118.

Instructions regarding War Diaries and Intelligence Summaries are contained in F. S. Regs., Part II. and the Staff Manual respectively. Title pages will be prepared in manuscript.

Place	Date	Hour	Summary of Events and Information	Remarks and references to Appendices
BAIZIEUX	Nov 1		2/3 Coy at BOUZINCOURT with R.E. Parts working at aerodrome	MSS.
"	2		do. Capt. THOM reported for duty	MSS.
"	3		do	MSS.
"	4		do	MSS.
"	5		do	MSS.
"	6		25 men at BUIRE with R.E.	MSS.
"	7		50 men at MERICOURT with R.E. & 25 men at RIBEMONT with R.E. 2/Lt Smith returned from leave	MSS.
"	8		50 men at MERICOURT with R.E. do.	MSS.
"	9		Capt. ROGERSON went on special leave. 50 men at MERICOURT with R.E. & 75 men at RIBEMONT	MSS.
"	10		25 men at RIBEMONT with R.E. Interior economy.	MSS.
"	11		do. 2/Lt Howie went on leave. 1/2 Coy at BOUZINCOURT with R.E. Draft of 10 men from Scotland.	MSS.
"	12		do	MSS.
"	13		do	MSS.
"	14		do Church service by Major Sinclair	MSS.

1577 Wt. W10791/1773 500,000 1/15 D. D. & L. A.D.S.S./Forms/C. 2118.

Army Form C. 2118.

WAR DIARY

INTELLIGENCE SUMMARY.

(Erase heading not required.)

Instructions regarding War Diaries and Intelligence Summaries are contained in F. S. Regs., Part II. and the Staff Manual respectively. Title pages will be prepared in manuscript.

Place	Date	Hour	Summary of Events and Information	Remarks and references to Appendices
BAIZIEUX	Nov 15		25 men at RIBEMONT with R.E. Interior Economy.	M.S.
" "	16		do. 25 men at BUIRE. Snowstorm.	M.S.
" "	17		½ Coy at BOUZINCOURT - Party at Sand pit at BAIZIEUX.	M.S.
" "	18		do. do.	
" "	19		2Lt HOWIE returned from leave do. 25 men at BUIRE. 25 men at RIBEMONT.	M.S.
" "	20		do. do.	
" "	21		do. Church service by MAJOR SINCLAIR do.	M.S.
" "	22		Interior Economy. do.	
" "	23		½ Coy at BOUZINCOURT. CAPT ROBERTSON returned from Extended Leave do.	M.S.
" "	24		do. do.	
" "	25		do. do.	M.S.
" "	26		do. do.	M.S.
" "	27		do. do.	M.S.
" "	28		do. Church service by MAJOR SINCLAIR. do.	M.S.
" "	29		Interior Economy do.	
" "	30		½ Coy at BOUZINCOURT do.	

bébé
(C)
Dae
Vol. VIII

WAR DIARY 51st Div. Cyclist Coy.
INTELLIGENCE SUMMARY
for DECEMBER

Army Form C. 2118.

Place	Date	Hour	Summary of Events and Information	Remarks and references to Appendices
BAIZIEUX	Dec 1		½ Coy at Bouzincourt with R.E. 25 men at Rosemont with R.E. 10 men at Sandpit	W.S.
"	2		do	W.S.
"	3		do	W.S.
"	4		do	W.S.
"	5		Interior Economy	W.S.
"	6		do	W.S.
"	7		½ Coy at Bouzincourt with RE	W.S.
"	8		do	W.S.
"	9		do	W.S.
"	10		do	W.S.
"	11		do	W.S.
"	12		do. Church parade by Major Sinclair do.	W.S.
"	13		Interior Economy. do	W.S.
"	14		½ Coy at Bouzincourt with RE do	W.S.
"	15		do do	W.S.
"	16		do do	W.S.

A. W. Rogerson, Capt.

Army Form C. 2118.

WAR DIARY
INTELLIGENCE SUMMARY.
(Erase heading not required.)

Instructions regarding War Diaries and Intelligence Summaries are contained in F. S. Regs., Part II. and the Staff Manual respectively. Title pages will be prepared in manuscript.

Place	Date	Hour	Summary of Events and Information	Remarks and references to Appendices
BAIZIEUX	DEC 17		1/2 Coy at BOUZINCOURT with R.E. 25 men at RIBEMONT with R.E. Capt. TAYLOR went on 8 days leave	A.P.
"	18		do. do. 10 men at Sandpit	A.P.
"	19		do. Church service by Canon VARINGS. do.	A.P.
"	20		Interior Economy do.	A.P.
"	21		83 men at RIBEMONT with R.E.	A.P.
"	22		do.	A.P.
"	23		do.	A.P.
"	24		Tactical scheme prepared but cancelled owing to weather. Interior Economy	A.P.
"	25		Interior Economy	A.P.
"	26	11am	Reft BAIZIEUX for MIRVAUX.	A.P.
"	27		Interior Economy	A.P.
MIRVAUX	27		do.	A.P.
"	28		do.	A.P.
"	29		Company Training	A.P.
"	30		Company Training	A.P.
"	31		do. Draft of 10 men from SCOTLAND.	A.P.

A.W. Rogerson, Capt.

51800 Due Cypeline Co.

Tom IX

Army Form C. 2118

WAR DIARY OF 51st DIVISIONAL CYCLIST COY.

INTELLIGENCE SUMMARY

(Erase heading not required.)

for JANUARY 1916

Instructions regarding War Diaries and Intelligence Summaries are contained in F.S. Regs., Part II. and the Staff Manual respectively. Title Pages will be prepared in manuscript.

Place	Date	Hour	Summary of Events and Information	Remarks and references to Appendices
MIRVAUX	Jan 1		Interior Economy.	K.S.
"	2		Company Training. Church service by Major Burns. Lce Corpl. AMcLEOD gazetted 2Lt 2/5th SEAFORTHS	K.S.
"	3		Company Training.	
"	4		do	K.S.
"	5		do	
"	6		do	K.S.
"	7		Draft of 1 man from SCOTLAND.	
"	8		Interior Economy. Repairing billets	
"	9		do Church service by Major Burns	K.S.
"	10		Company Training. 2Lt HOWIE and 1 platoon reconnoitring rutdown. Div. Area.	
"	11		Draft of 2 men from Scot. do	K.S.
"	12		Tactical Scheme do	
"	13		Company Route March. 2 platoons with 153rd Brigade in tactical scheme near FLASCELLES.	K.S.
"	14		Company Training.	
"	15		do Repairing billets & preparing horse standings.	K.S.
"	16		Interior Economy. do Church service by Major Burns.	

A. W. Rogerson, Capt.

Army Form C. 2118

WAR DIARY of 51st DIVISIONAL CYCLIST COY.
INTELLIGENCE SUMMARY
(Erase heading not required.)

for JANUARY 1916

Place	Date	Hour	Summary of Events and Information	Remarks and references to Appendices
MIRVAUX	JAN 17		Company Training. Tactical Scheme.	W.S.
"	18		Company Training. Interior Economy.	W.S.
"	19		do	W.S.
"	20		do	W.S.
"	21		2 platoons with 152nd BRIG. and 4 platoons with 154th BRIG. in Tactical Scheme	W.S.
"	22		Interior Economy. BATHS. Preparing horse standings. Preparing billets.	W.S.
"	23		do. Churchservice by MAJOR BURNS. Draft of 7 men from Scot. Lt. Crooks went on leave.	W.S.
"	24		1/2 Coy training and 1/2 Coy making horse standings	W.S.
"	25		Tactical Scheme. do	W.S.
"	26		1/2 Coy with 152nd BRIG. in tactical scheme. 1/2 Coy preparing horse standings.	W.S.
"	27		2 platoons with 154th BRIGADE. do	W.S.
"	28		Company Training. do	W.S.
"	29		Interior Economy. Baths.	W.S.
"	30		do. Church service by MAJOR BURNS.	W.S.
"	31		Company Training	W.S.

A. W. Rogerson Capt.

WAR DIARY

INTELLIGENCE SUMMARY

(Erase heading not required.)

Army Form C. 2118

WAR DIARY for FEBRUARY 1916
INTELLIGENCE SUMMARY of 51st DIV. CYCLIST COY.

Vol X

Place	Date	Hour	Summary of Events and Information	Remarks and references to Appendices
MIRVAUX	Feb. 1		Company Training. Practising digging themselves in.	MS.
"	2		Route march.	
"	3		Company Training. 2t. MAITLAND left for ENGLAND to join his unit.	MS.
"	4		Interior Economy. Lecture on Smoke Helmets by Capt. MELVIN of 1/2 F.Amb.	
"	5		BATHS. Interior Economy.	MS.
"	6		Kit inspection. Church Service by MAJOR BURNS. Lt SMITH went on leave.	MS.
"	7		Company Fatigues	MS.
DAOURS	8		Coy moved to DAOURS.	
"	9		Interior Economy. Fatigues.	MS
"	10		Company Training. Draft of 6 men from SCOTLAND.	
"	11		Reconnaissance of Roads in BRAY Area.	MS
"	12		do	
"	13		do	
"	14		Interior Economy. Capt. ROGERSON went on special leave	MS
"	15		do. Inspection of Smoke helmets.	
"	16		Company Training. & Lecture on Cyclist work.	MS
"	17		do Baths.	
"	18		Interior Economy & repairing Spokes.	MS

M Taylor Capt.

WAR DIARY of 51st DIV. CYCLIST COY.

INTELLIGENCE SUMMARY for FEBRUARY

Army Form C. 2118

(Erase heading not required.)

Instructions regarding War Diaries and Intelligence Summaries are contained in F. S. Regs., Part II. and the Staff Manual respectively. Title Pages will be prepared in manuscript.

Place	Date	Hour	Summary of Events and Information	Remarks and references to Appendices
DAOURS	Feb 19		Medical inspection of Coy. Fatigues. 2Lts GRANT & HOWIE on road reconnaissance	N.S.
"	20		Church parade. Interior Economy. do. of BRAY Area	N.S.
"	21		Route march 10 men with R.E. CAPT THOM [Inven?] on leave to SCOT.	N.S.
"	22		Company Training 30 men + 1 Officer with R.E. cutting brushwood	N.S.
"	23		do do	
"	24		do do	
"	25		do do	N.S.
"	26		do do	
"	27		Church parade. Interior Economy. do	N.S.
"	28		Fatigues. Orders to move on 29th do	N.S.
"	29		Coy. proceeded to FLESSELLES	N.S.

A.A. Taylor Capt.

51

Cyclist Coy
Vol XI

WAR DIARY of 51st Div. Cyclist Coy. Army Form C. 2118

INTELLIGENCE SUMMARY

for MARCH 1916.

(Erase heading not required.)

Instructions regarding War Diaries and Intelligence Summaries are contained in F. S. Regs., Part II. and the Staff Manual respectively. Title Pages will be prepared in manuscript.

Place	Date	Hour	Summary of Events and Information	Remarks and references to Appendices
FLESSELLES	March 1		Fatigue & Interior Economy.	A/S
"	2		Route march.	A/S
"	3		Interior Economy.	A/S
"	4		do. Company paid.	A/S
"	5		do	A/S
HARDINVAL	6	9 am.	Coy moved to HARDINVAL	A/S
"	7		Interior Economy.	A/S
OPPY	8	5 pm	Coy moved to OPPY arrived 3 pm.	A/S
MAROEUIL	9	8.5"	Coy moved to MAROEUIL arrived 5 pm.	A/S
"	10	4 pm	Coy moved into trenches at A.23 (Ref. Map 51 B) with 4 "Seaforth" H.Qs.	
TRENCHES	11		2 platoons in front line & 4 platoons in support line. Quiet day.	
"	12		do. Repairing & deepening do. Stormy weather. Trenches very muddy.	A/S
"	13		do. trenches. Parapets do. Improvement in weather.	A/S
"	14		do. very weak. Much do. 1 man wounded in head.	A/S
"	15		do. work was spent on do.	A/S
"	16		do. strengthening them. do. 1 man wounded in head.	A/S
			do more activity from Enemys Trench mortars & Artillery.	

Capen Capt
O.P. 51st Div Cyclist Coy

WAR DIARY of 51st DIV. CYCLIST COY
for MARCH
INTELLIGENCE SUMMARY

Army Form C. 2118

(Erase heading not required.)

Place	Date	Hour	Summary of Events and Information	Remarks and references to Appendices
RESERVE TRENCHES ROCLINCOURT	MARCH 17	7 pm	Coy left front trenches & proceeded to Reserve Trenches at ECURIE & ROCLINCOURT	A09
"	18	10.45 pm	Capt. ROGERSON wounded in arm by bullet. Lt C.T. McWILLIAM killed by bullet.	A08
"	19		Working parties with 4th SEAFORTHS & 4th GORDONS - opening up old trenches	A05
"	20		Working parties with 9th ROYAL SCOTS, 4th SEAFORTHS & 4th GORDONS "	A06
"	21		Working parties with 9th ROYAL SCOTS & 4th GORDONS - do	A06
			Draught of 3 men from Scot-	
FRONT TRENCHES	22		Went into trenches with 4th SEAFORTHS. Occupies same part as previously. 1 platoon in front line. 4 platoons in Support. & 1 in reserve -	A07
"	23		do	A08
"	24		Coy busy repairing & strengthening parapet, laying trench boards, deepening trench & opening up Communication trench.	A08
"	25		do	A08
"	26		do	A08
"	27		do	A08
"	28	9 pm	Coy left trenches at 9 pm - arrives MAROEUIL at 2 am. proceeds to HERMAVILLE	A08
HERMAVILLE	29		Fatigues	A08
"	30		do 1 Officer & 30 men with 8th ROYAL SCOTS repairing trench north of MAROEUIL	A08
"	31		2 Officers & 80 men with 1/1 R.E. making light railway at AUX RIETZ do - Colin Bell Capt 6° 51st Div Cyclist C	

57

Cyclist Coy

Vol XII

Army Form C. 2118

WAR DIARY
of 51st DIV. CYCLIST COY.
INTELLIGENCE SUMMARY for APRIL.

(Erase heading not required.)

Instructions regarding War Diaries and Intelligence Summaries are contained in F. S. Regs., Part II. and the Staff Manual respectively. Title Pages will be prepared in manuscript.

Place	Date	Hour	Summary of Events and Information	Remarks and references to Appendices
HERMAVILLE	APRIL 1		44 men with ½ R.E. at AUXRIETZ making trench for light railway.	
"	2		30 men clearing Territorial Trench.	
"	3		2/3 Coy at AUX RIETZ with ½ F. Coy. R.E. - 30 men in Territorial Trench. Tactical Scheme with 17th CORPS mounted troops	
"	4		2/3 Coy at AUX RIETZ & 30 men in Territorial Trench.	
"	5		do 30 men with D.A.D.O.S. One man wounded	
"	6		do Draft of 3 men from SCOTLAND	
"	7	3 pm	do	
"	8	7.30 pm	do Draft of 10 men from Base.	
"	9		Church Service do by Major Sinclair	
"	10	7.30 pm	do	
"	11	3 pm	do	
"	12		do Officers & N.C.O.s at Flammenwerfer Exhibition	
"	13		do	
"	14		Baths at MAROEUIL. 12 men at Bombing Course with 6th ARGYLL & SUTH. HGS	
"	15		30 men received instruction in do -	

Infantry at HERMAVILLE from CAPT ROWBOTTOM.

J.M. Smith Lt.
for O.C.

WAR DIARY of 51st DIV. CYCLIST COY.

INTELLIGENCE SUMMARY for APRIL

Army Form C. 2118

Place	Date	Hour	Summary of Events and Information	Remarks and references to Appendices
MAROEUIL TRENCHES	16		Left HERMAVILLE at 9.30 A.M. Arrived MAROEUIL at 11. Left for trenches at 1.30 p.m. with 6th ARG. & SUTH. HGS. Arrived in Support trenches in LABYRINTH at 5 p.m. 2Lt. WALKER (6th SEAFORTH HLGs) attached for bombing officer.	AS
"	17		Working parties in support & front line trenches	AS
"	18	11 A.M.	Heavy bombardment of our Support trenches. 2 men slightly wounded. 2 men seriously wounded	AS
"	19	10 P.M.	Coy relieved Right Coy of 6 A.& S. HGs on front line. One man died of wounds	AS
"	20		Repairing damage done to trenches. Exchange of bombs with GERMANS at Sap P.3.	AS
"	21		2 men wounded. Weather very unsettled. Trenches very muddy.	AS
"	22	5 p.m.	Coy relieved by 8th A & S. HLGs. 2Lt. D. LINDSAY reported for duty.	AS
HERMAVILLE	23	11 A.M.	Coy bathed at MAROEUIL DIV. BATHS. arrived MAROEUIL 8.30 p.m. Coy left for HERMAVILLE 3 p.m.	AS
"	24		Interior Economy. 2Lt. GRANT went to Div. Bombing Course at HERMAVILLE	AS
"	25		100 men working at Div. Grenade School. 12 men receiving instruction in bombing from 2Lt. WALKER	AS
"	26		do. 2Lt. WALKER returned to his unit	AS
"	27		Tactical Scheme at TERNAS with N.I.H. for Officers & N.C.O.s	AS
"	29		Coy went into trenches with 6th A.& S. HLGs relieving Right Coy of 8th A.& S. HLGs in front line	AS
"	30		2 men wounded. Repairing trenches etc	AS

JWSmith
for O.C.